Out of the Maze Into the Labyrinth

A Collection of Personal Essays

Virginia A. Ward

authorHOUSE®

AuthorHouse™
1663 Liberty Drive
Bloomington, IN 47403
www.authorhouse.com
Phone: 1-800-839-8640

Published by AuthorHouse 10/22/2012

ISBN: 978-1-4772-6747-9 (sc)
ISBN: 978-1-4772-6746-2 (e)

Table of Contents

Acknowledgments

Thank you valued friends, writers all, for your expertise and time in enabling the author to complete this book.

Luci Bailey
Linda Holland Glick
Jo-Anne Hines
Beverly Miller
Marcelle Mignault-Strong
Hana Whitfield

The Power of the Labyrinth and the Personal Essay

When I first began writing I had no plan, no great work in mind. I only knew I liked the feel of the pen in my hand and the page once I had scribbled words upon it.

Those who aspire to write are often afraid of journaling because it lays the self bare. I was one of those, but as I grew the writing grew with me, the journal entries more fluent. The word **journal** comes from Latin meaning *daily record*. It can be a diary, a chronicle of daily happenings, a record of memories or your thoughts on current history. The journal can be a ruled pad of paper, a memory book, a scrapbook, a small notebook kept in pocket or purse, etc.

Later in my life I discovered the labyrinth. With that knowledge I began to journal my feelings, frustrations, successes and, yes, my failures, more openly.

~~~

1. The personal essay has a **voice** -- the writer's voice. She or he writes in the first person (I) and is not compelled to look into the readers thoughts, but into the <u>writer's own thoughts.</u>

2. The **form** of personal essays lie in the writer's sharing of his or her experience in story form using the five (5) elements of story construction – theme, character, plot, setting, and point of view, experience that brings the personal essay to life for the reader.

3. **Truth** in a personal essay lies in the writer's ability to convey **truth** too the reader. Truth may not always be recognized by the reader but truth must always be evident in the story.

In Brief: Putting Pen to Paper

FOCUS:

(a) Choose an experience, a topic to write about.

(b) Relax, close your eyes. Concentrate on the event in terms of scenes and the elements (parts) of scenes; theme, character, plot, setting, point-of-view.

(c) Next list the events as they occurred.

(d) Then writing in scenes **show** what occurred through the event.

(e) Edit, refine your work. Evaluate your focus, your purpose.

CONTENT:

(f) Ask yourself, "Have I communicated my purpose adequately?"

(g) Do I have enough information? Have I researched my theme adequately?

ORGANIZATION:

(h) Does the writing flow logically from my topic/ purpose.

(i) Will my organization make it easy for readers to follow.

(j) Am I sure I considered grammar, spelling, word choice, sentence structure and any other things relevant to my essay.

The Beauty of Labyrinth Writing

Begin exactly where you are located. Take out your pad and pen. Write anything. Your focus will become clear.

Experience what's happening around you here and now.

Write without thinking.

Give yourself permission to write the worst junk in the universe.

Let feelings arise and spill on the page without judgment or censure.

Don't be afraid of what you write. You can edit it later.

ALSO BY VIRGINIA A.WARD

Aching Heart – Burning Soul
Surviving Catholicism
(a memoir)

Kitchen Table Tales
(a memoir)

Threads
(a novel)

Writing Memoir: Step-by-Step

Writing Short Story: Step-by-Step

Writing Short Fiction: Step-by-Step
(An instructional guide for Young Authors)

Discovery

"The real voyage of discovery consists not in seeking new landscapes but in having new eyes." Marcel Proust

Labyrinths. Beneath the maple trees, year upon year I saw them, two bulky balls of cord each set two feet apart forming a path on the lawn of Skidmore College campus. Women in peasant dresses, others in odd assortments of tie-died ankle length skirts and message t-shirts walking the labyrinth's path, a throwback to their flower child days? I saw them and asked myself, "How can inspiration come from this?"

The International Women's Writing Guild conferences taught me many things about the art of writing, but I continued to shake my head at those who persisted in walking the labyrinth's path.

My husband and I once visited Sholom Park, a small jewel among many in Central Florida. The park's pond, with its fountain and trail, were scenic. He would have wandered further, but I saw no reason to linger. So we left, not having explored other trails, or the Garden Walk. Nor did we stop to take a brochure from the box near visitor parking.

A year later, a friend called and suggested we visit Sholom before going to lunch. I didn't really want to visit the park. I'd been there and had no desire to return. But Linda, an artist, had visited often. Her enthusiasm was contagious, my curiosity aroused. She became my guide.

She picked up a brochure, opened it, and pointed to the labyrinth's map location. We walked the path that day, she pointing out views that begged for contemplation, I discovering the wonder of it all. The following day we revisited Sholom, taking photographs of each stop along the path; the pond, the water lilies, the foot bridge, the benches, trees, flowers…

Over time, in my mind's eye, I began to see why the women of Skidmore walked the labyrinth's path. Some say the *labyrinth* is a metaphor for life's Journey; that as you walk you may experience enlightenment. For others praying as one strolls relieves anxiety and quiets one's fears.

Labyrinths: Origin and Meaning

"The beautiful thing about learning
is nobody can take it away from you."
B. B. King

I long believed that labyrinth and maze were interchangeable terms. I've learned that isn't so.

The maze is a tour puzzle constructed with an intricate network of pathways and dead ends. Its focus centers on the presentation of numerous options from which the traveler selects direction and, having chosen, employs a strategy to overcome confusion and find the uninterrupted path.

In its pure form, the labyrinth, on the other hand, has a single uninterrupted path that winds and shifts to the center and back. There are no dead ends or crossed paths to confuse the voyager and only one entrance and exit.

Where the function of the maze is about the exterior life, the essence of the labyrinth is interior; guidance, trust and reflection. Labyrinths represent the journey of life; in the center one slows and listens, then returns to the outer world renewed.

Meandering is a term often used for walking a labyrinth. It is reminiscent of a lazy river as it bends this way and that on its way to the sea. As the river pokes along its course, the visitor slows over the path's distance. Just as the river calms, the pilgrim finds quiet. Water and humanity join in sacred space.

§

The history of labyrinths, which have no geographic, cultural, or religious limit, reach into prehistory. But as medieval times passed, the spiritual uses of labyrinths were forgotten and fell into disuse. Many were destroyed between the seventeenth and nineteenth centuries: carvings, tablets, mosaics, manuscripts …. In recent years the labyrinth has reemerged as a "new" spiritual tool; a more modernistic mode of worship. Whatever their origin these enigmas have brought a sense of peace, comfort, and rest to those who stop to meditate within their space.

This traveler, once a skeptic, a doubter no more.

The International Women's Writing Guild's commitment to the concept of the labyrinth is found in its members creativity, fostering feelings of belonging and inspiration, its celebration of one's passion for the written word, for passing to members the nuts and bolts of writing practice, and encouraging the writer to explore new approaches to all aspects of the writing profession.

Solitude and Peace

Never, for the sake of peace and quiet, deny your own experience or convictions." Dag Hammarskjöld

Early morning, silent, tranquil. I absorb the sun's face hidden in blankets of mist over mountain tops. On the island's shore, a lone boat rests at anchor while its captain dreams below.

On the water's edge green shoots peek from tree branches. Those fully open reach to the heavens waiting to cast shade on those beneath.

Later now, small birds fly, chasing one another beyond the beach in ancient ritual while I lay earthbound.

The morning silence is broken by roaring engines as a boat's pilot races his craft over the water's surface sending ripples toward the water's edge.

The mist lifts. Mountain tops blink at the rays of the rising sun, and wink to the water below.

So the day begins.

§

The spirit welcomes solitude. Inside myself is a place where I live unaccompanied, a place where I float in ever-flowing springs of possibility. Having left the chaos of the outer world behind, I enter the inner world. I ponder, consider, reflect on my life within; mind, sense, being. I examine the relationships, attitudes, values, and spirituality that resides in the core of my being.

From the time I was very young, I consciously sought solitude, unaware of the life I was entering. I didn't recognize or know then what this state of seclusion, of isolation, meant or that what I was experiencing was either good or bad. Rather, it was for me a way of getting away from the noise that filled the house; the tension, the multi-generational clashes, threats and recriminations of my daily existence.

I spent a lot of time, particularly on weekends, during school breaks and summer vacations, fantasying about my ideal existence and writing stories about the life I would have one day. My parents never saw that part of me. They saw me only as a *social butterfly*. And I *was* busy. But as social as I seemed to be, I often felt out of place – that I didn't in. Nor was I considered very bright. In later years I came to see myself as quite capable.

When I went to my desk to write, or sat in the window seat of my room looking out over the back yard or across the hedge of pine trees between our house and the next door neighbor, my mind drifted and I began to write in one of the spiral notebooks where I kept the tales that came to me. I don't know where those pages are or if they still exist; I lost track of them long ago.

Solitude can be painful for the young, but I don't remember feeling uncomfortable. During times alone, in my youth and beyond, I have never lacked things upon which to focus my mind. There was my writing, of course, and I was also an avid reader. Beginning in my early teens, I borrowed from bookshelves lined with the volumes Mother had enjoyed – Zane Gray, James Oliver Curwood, Rida Johnson Young and more. My tastes advanced as I grew older but now, in my seventies, I seek out those yellowed pages now and then.

Somewhere along the way my pen grew still. The demands of my life required I attend to other things. I'd written all my life, but not the books I dreamed I'd author. Writing was a large part of my work; manuals and curricula, handbooks and position papers – the list goes on. Then, toward the end of my career, life took yet another turn, as it is wont to do and I found myself longing for the kind of writing I had planned to produce so many years before. With that came a commitment to encourage students to realize their gifts. And as they grew they began to smile, to participate, to feel better about themselves....

Solitude, removal to a place where concentration, reflection, meditation comes more easily, may be physical but the desired result requires time and patience. As the ability to resist distraction mounts, mental seclusion engages an inner life, the ability to become absorbed in thought.

Sholom Park's labyrinth is a peaceful place tucked away in the hush of nature. Along the path one is likely to find an artist painting wild flowers, a musician sitting on the lawn softly playing her instrument, or a poet beside the lily pond framing his latest work and under a moss covered oak a wounded soul seeking rest. However many times I transit the path there are always new revelations to enrich the inner being, the soul.

Greener Grass

"*The grass is always greener on the other side of the fence.*

First translated from Latin to English by Richard Traverner."

It is difficult to ascertain the origins of proverbs — brief statements that convey obvious truths. Erasmus, Dutch writer, scholar and humanist wrote in Latin about the discontent of one man toward another's good fortune, but it was Richard Traverner in 1545 who published the English translation. "*The corn in an other mans ground semeth euer more fertyll and plentifull than doth oure owne.*"

The message is ages old. There are those who are never satisfied with their situation. They see others circumstances as more desirable than their own.

Plainly, this ancient saying refers to the inability of humankind to be content with what one has.

I close my eyes and breathe in the sweetness of the early

summer air. I gaze across calm waters to the mountains and contemplate what has been, what is, and what is yet to be.

§

I was a child of the 1940's. Although very young, I have vivid memories of the World War II era: air raid sirens, blackouts, rationing, and overheard conversations of my mother's over the back yard fence. I remember Mrs. Peters with fondness. A much older woman than my mother, Mrs. Peters kept a flag in her living-room window for each of her three sons. Through the war years she lived with the concern, the fear, that one or all three would not come home.

Mrs. Peters was a scrubbed and polished gray-haired woman with a furrowed brow, toughened palms, and a slight limp on her right side. She was always ready to lend a hand, to help a neighbor, to share the bounty of her fruit and vegetable gardens. She smiled when she spoke to my mother over the fence or handed me an armful of rhubarb for pie, or a pan full of currents for jam.

What she held most dear had nothing to do with *things*. She valued her family, her country and prayed for an end to the war. Though she never spoke of it, I had a feeling Mrs. Peters by far cared more for her side of the fence than any other.

During those years our parents kept my sister and I shielded from fear. I knew Dad worried about his cousins fighting in Europe and the Pacific. He was concerned, too, for my aging grandparents and their safety; they were of German descent and not popular with some.

§

Then one day, as the clock chimed twelve, my sister and I, as usual, hurried to the kitchen for lunch and found Mom sitting on the floor, her legs curled under her body, her eyes streaming with tears.

The picture remains vivid, so does the fright I felt.

I remember that I said, "Mommy, are you hurt?"

"No," she said through her tears. "Listen to the radio. The war is over." And tears continued to flow down her cheeks.

We stood staring, not knowing what to do. We had never seen our mother cry as she did that day. Being so young I didn't realize that there were those who didn't cry only in sadness, but in times of joy as well.

Much has come and gone since that long ago day and as each year has passed I morn the loss of what was; walking the streets after dark alone and without fear, not viewing every male I met with suspicion, looking forward to my fourteenth birthday and being a babysitter, anticipating my sixteenth birthday – getting my driver's license and a steady after-school job, going to the bank where I put most of what I earned in savings and a bit in my pocket … Along the way I rejected excess and learned what responsibility and accountability meant, and as I did I grew from child to adult.

I've been told countless times that it's a new age, a new world; I need to lighten up, rid myself of rigidity, embrace the *new freedom*, join the pack. But I could not and cannot, as some have suggested, be *fixed*. The code that governs my life – fundamental truths that distinguish the difference between right and wrong – have deep roots within my core.

§

I'm reminded of *The Picture of Dorian Gray*, written by Oscar Wilde in the late nineteenth century. The novel's theme is the pursuit of self-indulgence.

An artist paints a portrait of the very handsome Dorian Gray, who subsequently has a conversation with a gentleman in the artist's garden. Dorian is fascinated by the man's world view, the pursuit of "beauty." Since his beauty will one day fade Dorian concludes that the pursuit of beauty is a worthy undertaking. He goes so far as to wish that his portrait age rather than he himself.

Sometime later, he looks at himself in the painting and sees that his face has a scornful expression. His wish has been granted. Over the next eighteen years Dorian samples depravity upon depravity.

Ultimately Dorian kills a man. Frightened, he promises to change his life. But before long he abandons his promise. When he looks at the portrait once more, the painting has again become grotesque.

Infuriated, Dorian slashes the painting.

Later servants find Dorian's body. He has been stabbed. His body, suddenly old, and grisly, is a gruesome thing lying beside the painting while the portrait has returned to its original form.

§

The point? Through time it has been a weakness of human beings to desire the greener grass one perceives on another's side of the fence, just as Dorian Gray pursued the life that had been opened to him by a stranger. I have not been immune to this imperfection. Yet I've found that the closer I come to what I first perceived as greener grass, the clearer vision emerges and I observe the ideal flawed as seen from a distance.

When I was in fourth grade it was the teacher's practice to have the class sing happy birthday to each student on his or her special day. I could barely wait for my turn to shine, to be recognized, to have the class clap in celebration for me. But when the day arrived and I was invited to stand in front of the room while the class sang, some of my classmates snickered at me. That the teacher brought order to the incident didn't take away my embarrassment or heal my hurt. I had been rejected by my classmates.

I wasn't part of a clique. I wasn't from the *right* family. I didn't live in a pricey neighborhood, or hang around with the *right* kids. I was gangly and awkward. I was embarrassed and in humiliation I learned that what you desire, what appears to be so special, can in reality be fantasy. When I arrived home my dad was there and I told him what happened. We had a snack and talked about my special day and I began to think about the cake I knew Mom had hidden in the dining room. I learned a lot about greener pastures that day.

As I progressed through school I was to learn other lessons that reinforced earlier experiences. As I grew older I took a fancy to Mercedes-Benz automobiles. The time came when my husband and I explored purchasing such an automobile. It didn't take more than a few minutes in the driver's seat to realize that the seat was uncomfortable and the vehicle cramped. When I shut the door it sounded tinny and the finish work didn't justify the price. Were any of the mechanisms to fail it would be expensive to fix. I learned once again that the greener pasture was not as lovely close up as it appeared to be at a distance.

Having grown up in the World War II period through the mid-fifties, my character and value system is solidly anchored in the Greatest Generation; dedication to family, the sanctity of marriage, respect for others and for authority, accountability, responsibility, modesty, acceptance of who I am – both the love and the flawed. I was expected to take life seriously, to accept the premise that men went to work and women took care of home and children.

But as the fifties ended and the sixties began, a new generation, the Baby Boomers came solidly into place. The ideology, morality and value system previously passed to children by family members began to disappear. The taboos of the 1950's were not only tolerated, but wholly accepted by the new genesis. It is generally believed that this happened because Boomers, as the children of the sixties through the nineties became known, were taught by the news media rather than family members. But that explanation seems too simple for such a complex phenomenon.

Nevertheless, as this period population became self-absorbed, their narcissism became so extreme that the Boomer generation was divided into several sub-groups. Subsequent to the Greatest Generation was the Silent Generation of the fifties, followed by the Boomer Generation of the sixties with its Generation Gap. The adolescents of the seventies became ever more alienated from the past and by the eighties, negligent parents had contributed to modeling the first wave of wayward youth, Generation X.

The Boomer population's morals and values continue to become ever more corrupt than those that preceded them, leading to a further debasement of society. The innocent fashion of the 1950's gave way to miniskirts, low-cut blouses, bare midriffs, and ever unfolding nudity. The Generation Gap, between the Greatest Generation and the Boomers, was far greater than that between the Boomers and their children. The Boomers threw out the morals and standards of their parents. Their existence was self-centered, based on self-indulgence; drugs, alcohol, free-love, instant gratification, compulsive behavior, no concept of providing for a rainy day, the list goes on. Boomers seem never to have matured. One generation melted into another, so much so that it is often difficult to discern where one generation ends and the other begins.

As parents began making decisions based on what their children wanted rather than on what was best for the child, authority shifted to the child and parents became powerless.

Perhaps the Millennial age, Generation Y, children of the Boomers, may begin to reverse the downward spiral of our culture. The Boomers seem to learn little as they age and can never claim the authority the Greatest Generation commanded. It is generally felt that it is the Millennial Generation to whom the Greatest Generation will hand the cloak of authority.

So we come full circle. As for me, I have never found greener pastures, nor have those born in the latter half of the twentieth century. Perhaps I didn't look hard enough. Am I doomed to search evermore? I think not. Greener pastures have been under my feet all the time.

Reaching for the Light

"Dare to reach out your hand into the darkness to pull another hand into the light." Norman B. Rice

I strain to grasp the light, to capture its glow and settle it on my world. I press against the darkness, the forces that cause flowers to wilt and trees to withhold shady resting places. After a storm I study the half circle of the rainbow, let my imagination trace its full circle and reflect on its promise. I remember a story I was told as a child; of the rainbow, the symbol of the Great Flood and of the promised undoing of misery.

I observe the lotus blossom. As evening approaches it closes its petals and lies on the water. In the morning it stretches, rises from the mud and opens above the surface. Oh, that it was so for mortals.

The light eludes me. In today's world, for me and those like me, there is no rainbow promise, no lotus blossom rising. The values, morals, and ethics that govern our personal and global lives have expired. We are passé, out of date, antiques, throwbacks to what has become, an over the counter-cultural era born in the 1960's, a steady downward degradation that includes the loss of personal dignity, moral and intellectual character. Many of us are seen as rigid personalities. Among some that translates to "unstable" personalities. After all, we are incapable of adapting to this new age. We are ungracious, inflexible, uncompromising, stiff and dense; we just *don't get it*.

§

In that other time there were specific principles to learn from parents. Entering the next generation, I was eager to pass on to my children the cultural values I had been taught. But the generational disruptions experienced after World War II condemned many of us to lose what we had held most dear.

Moral courage, even in the face of personal consequences, disappeared. Honesty took a back seat to lying, stealing and cheating. Integrity, once valued as the hallmark of a principled person, died. Personal responsibility became a game in which calamity was always someone else's fault. Respecting others often turned to bullying. Civility became the right to embarrass and humiliate others at the least infraction. Sacrifice in the interest of others or a cause was replaced by the "*me*" phenomenon of self-centeredness and self-indulgence. Fairness – the idea that rules are applied impartially – became self-interest first. Cooperation faded with compromise. Good-enough became a substitute for hard work and instant gratification took the place of patience. The inventory of the lost seems endless. For example, faithfulness, independence, tolerance, and self-respect have yet to be probed.

§

Traditionally faithfulness was fostered within the family. As a child I was aware of a connection, a link, to the past and another to the future. From conception I anticipated the arrival of my children. My husband and I set aside a room for the nursery. We looked forward to baby showers and soon after birth to introducing our child to the spiritual world.

As time went on we taught each of our children an ethical code that included respecting parents and siblings, extended family and friends.

As parents we strove to expose our children to playmates of families who shared our values. In school, children were expected to pay attention in class and we were diligent in reinforcing each child's strengths.

During the teen years our children were expected to perform the duties asked of them, to contribute to family life, and to be attentive in school. Social activities were expected to be wider ranging, but within the rules set by family and society. In the environment provided by us, the parents, our children began to become self-aware, to develop personal identity, to be conscious of the personalities of those around them, and to form friendships based on ethics, not prejudices.

Our young continued to grow through high school and college. They built careers, married, and enriched the family tree. The cycle continued anew.

As in the Confucian philosophical approach to family life and structural relations, we assumed our culture would avoid lawlessness and that social problems would not touch us. It was those who lacked moral and social structure that found themselves enmeshed in anti-social behavior and lawlessness.

Faithfulness is commitment to family and loyalty to friends. Faithfulness rests on the foundation of ethics and morals one develops in the family. But if that is not to be, where is the light? It arrives each morning bringing warmth, solace and the hope of never-ending new beginnings.

§

Independence, the right of an individual to decide how one will live one's life, was once shaped around the interactions between parents and children. Today many of us find ourselves in the midst of an explosion of estrangement.

In each generation we must accept the proposition that each child has the right to direct his/her life as he/she wishes. It is their live, after all.

Each of us has the right to make that decision. If a child lives in ways we would not choose that is the parent's issue, not the child's. If a child blames others for unwise selections, the child made the choices. We cannot control others. It is useless to try. Just as the parent did, each child spends his/her life as he/she chooses. But a child does not have the right to demand a parent, or parents, accept a child's choices unconditionally.

The dislocation in the *new* culture is, in many ways, foreign to earlier generations. While parents strive to accommodate a child's preferences we are not bound to accept them. At some point each young person is responsible for his/her indiscretions and the consequences of their acts.

Where is the light? It sometimes remains in shadow until we take another path, or separate ourselves from an unsustainable position.

§

Tolerance recognizes and respects differences among people. The difficulty is that each of us demands tolerance for self, but many do not hold this principal valid for others.

The Greatest Generation recognizes that cultural changes have not been the sole fault of the Boomers. Some remaining from the Greatest Generation have become as spoiled, selfish, materialistic and morally bankrupt as their children.

Society is forced to care for, or accommodate, those who do not care for themselves without any distinction made for those whose own choices led them to their downfall, as opposed to those mentally or physically unfit for the task.

The responsible majority sacrifices and does without so that others have in some cases more or as much as those who do without by choice. As time passes society feels foolish, becomes angry and totally unappreciated for their giving.

So, where is the light? Each of us, if we have not totally squandered our gifts, have a bottom line, a point at which we say *no more*; live as you wish and I will follow the path I choose. Should our paths converge in moments of grace, value the calm, value its worth. Yet, if there is no good-will move on, leaving behind the unfilled promise of so long ago and strive always toward the glow beyond the clouds.

§

Self- esteem and self-respect seem similar but there is a difference. Over the stages of the *new* generation's lives, parents and teachers focused on the self-esteem of children and said little about respect. Self-esteem was *the* solution offered for all our children's problems. Praise them, whether they deserve it or not.

Defined, self-esteem is thinking well of one's self. Self-respect, on the other hand, fosters respect for others which, in turn, fosters respect of self. In other words, to receive respect we must first learn to give it to others.

Growing up being told how great you are doesn't make you a desirable person to be around. Living by the Golden Rule, "Do unto others as you would have them do unto you," is a far better measure of the ability to form positive relationships with others and self than it is to be heaped with praise that may not be warranted.

There is a scarcity of self-respect in the *new* culture that knows no embarrassment or modesty. But the *Me*

Generation isn't focused so much on self-absorption as on setting a course for their lives that leaves behind the values and morals learned at their parents' knees and with the unshakable conviction that they are important and deserve to get what they want. But the reality of life's struggles, especially for the *Me Generation*, is that they get less than they expect because they demand so much, and less than previous generations because they are unable, or reluctant to accept the down-to-earth substance of existence. The *Me Generation* is straightforward and unapologetic about its self-focus and, at the same time, incapable of honest self-evaluation. The mantra of the *Me Generation* is *do what's best for me, what makes me happy, do what's best for me in all situations.*

Reach for the light. Among *Aesop's Fables* is the story of *The Peacock and the Goddess Juno.* The peacock went to Juno seeking to have the voice of a nightingale in addition to his beautiful plumage. Juno refused his request. The peacock was not appeased. He persisted by pointing out that he was her favorite bird. Juno's reply was, "Be content with what you have. One cannot be first in everything. And if your present wish were granted, you would soon find cause for fresh discontent."

Wounded Tree

*"If you have a wounded heart ...
there are only two remedies for
the suffering of the soul: hope and
patience."* Pythagoras

What could have caused such a wound? Each time I walk
the path I rest near *Wounded Tree*. It stands strong and
accepts its place. I study its scars and rough surface. I want
to stroke its gnarled bark, brush my hand across its broken
heart, console it, assure it that the hurt will pass, that its
spirit remains a symbol of the ability to endure. I am held
fast by the thought that this tree and I share the trauma
of loss and know the price we paid. All of us have been
stricken, including the greatest among us.

The tree stands statuesque against the sky. It has no
choice, no decision to make to save itself – what caused the
wound doesn't matter. Yet I suspect it was time, the beating
of tropical storms and the wind delivering sharp gusts
across the meadow that forced its bark to open, splintering

its trunk and forming its heart shaped wound. And still Wounded Tree survives, continuing to stand tall, reaching for the clouds. It shows new shoots in spring and shrugs off dying leaves in fall. It continues to shelter from the sun's heat and misting rain those who rest beneath its canopy. It stands as a symbol of survival, of the connection between humanity and nature, of its ability to persevere through time and space.

On the other hand, unlike Wounded Tree, I am complicit in my fate. Should I be self-satisfied because I held to principle, that I chose *the road less traveled*, in the end having carried a weighty burden, and leaving behind the companionship of humanity?

I exchanged that intimacy for the parched earth of morality and ethics. I am a ramrod; like the tree, unbending. I respect the right of others to select the choices they desire. But I have found that, in return, I am not extended the same prerogative.

I relate well to acquaintances and occasional companions, but have few contacts with which I can discuss a range of subjects openly, honestly. John Donne wrote, "No man is an island entire of it self; every man is a piece of the continent...."

Our secret places, the mechanisms we own by instinct and those we develop through experience, combine to create survival skills. How low do we bend, how deeply do we compromise, how frequently do we excuse, how often are we silent, how regularly do we ignore the immoral, the valueless, to maintain personal security and status?

Each time we turn from principle we scar our souls. In the beginning denying our principles leads us down the path of self–justification that ultimately brings us to a place called "go-along-to-get-along." The paradox is that when we stand on principle we are also scarred. At first we cling to principle, but as time goes on we become battle-weary, disillusioned, cynical, jaded. At some point we commit to principle.

Accepting that we are being unsuccessful, we begin the cycle of serving relationships, changing jobs, withdrawing from active participation and in social and professional organizations and events. Ore world becomes even smaller.

I understand the cost that adhering to principle brings. I first encountered it as a young teacher at St John's Middle School. The principal and staff were professional, caring and helpful. But within a few years the principal was moved and a new administrator was assigned to our building. We were sorry to see the change, but we were ready to work with the new director, Sister Noreen, and looked forward to the future.

As luck would have it the replacement was not what any of us had hoped for. She was unpleasant to students, unprofessional with colleagues and lacked the educational background and maturity one expected of a person in her position.

The situation finally came to a head. The disparity in how the two administrators treated teachers and staff caused tensions to rise and became difficult to explain to both students and parents.

There were those of us who lobbied for reason and change. Our suggestions were dismissed without study or consultation. A short time later I experienced the exercise of power and met its partner, "Evil."

St. Mark's, another religious school, was closing, and parents who could do so were anxious to enroll their children in Saint John's. It was obvious from the beginning that Sister Noreen was not happy about this influx of students. St. Mark's was only a short distance from Saint John's, but a world from the culture we had known.

Scars

*"There are chapters in every life that
are seldom read and certainly not
aloud." Carol Shields*

In addition to its defacement, Wounded Tree has a scar from
canopy to roots, the raised bark discolored and extending the
length of its trunk. I ask myself, "If these wounds were mine
what secrets would I hold beneath my disfigurement?"

Each of us has an inner life that we share with no one;
a life that others, no matter how intimate, never see. The
question becomes, by withholding what we learn from
experience do we deny life lessons to others? It's unfortunate
but true that one person's experience may evoke discomfort or
sympathy from another. But if two people have experienced
a similar trauma they may approach common ground.

Our secret places, the mechanisms we own by instinct
and those we develop through experience, combine to create
survival skills. How low do we bend, how deeply do we
compromise, how frequently do we excuse, how often are

we silent, how regularly do we ignore the immoral, the valueless, to maintain personal security and status?

Accepting that we are being unsuccessful, we begin the cycle of severing relationships, changing jobs, withdrawing from active participation in social and professional organizations and events. Our world becomes ever smaller.

I understand the cost that adhering to principle brings. I first encountered it as a young teacher at St. John's Middle School. The principal and staff were professional, caring and helpful. But within a few years the principal was moved and a new administrator was assigned to our building. We were sorry to see the change, but we were ready to work with the new director, Sister Noreen, and looked forward to the future.

As luck would have it the replacement was not what any of us had hoped for. She was unpleasant to students, unprofessional with colleagues, and lacked the educational background and maturity one expected of a person in her position.

The situation finally came to a head. The disparity in how the two administrators treated teachers and staff caused tensions to rise and became difficult to explain to both students and parents.

There were those of us who lobbied for reason and change. Our suggestions were dismissed without study or consultation. A short time later I experienced the exercise of power and met its partner, evil.

St. Mark's, another religious school, was closing, and parents who could do so were anxious to enroll their children in St. John's. It was obvious from the beginning that Sister Noreen was not happy about this influx of students. St Mark's was only a short distance from St. John's, but a world away from the culture we had known.

Not long after Sister Noreen came to St. John's I was

designated coordinator of the middle school. One morning she called me to her office for what I thought was to be a routine conversation. Without greeting or explanation I was told to expel one of the boys who had come to us from St. Mark's. I suggested that what she asked was not my place.

When I asked why she wanted him expelled she said, "I don't want *that* boy in my school." I had seen Sister Noreen in the hall earlier, scolding the boy. In that moment I knew Sister Noreen's motivation.

"Where are your shoes?" she asked. "You know you are not to wear sneakers to class. You may only wear them on the playground."

"I only have sneakers, Sister," he said with eyes downcast.

"Don't forget your shoes tomorrow."

"These are my shoes, Sister."

She looked at the boy, disgust on her face, then turned and left the twelve year old standing alone embarrassed and ashamed.

I walked the distance between us, patted the boy's back and told him to go to class.

I was enraged and, at the same time sad. He was to be expelled because his family couldn't afford to buy dress shoes. I took a deep breath and went to Sister Noreen's office. I looked across her desk and said, "If you want that child expelled, Sister, you'll have to do it yourself."

That being said, I turned and left her sitting there. Over the time that followed I was harassed regularly by this woman of God. I decided to leave St. John's before the school year ended.

That experience taught me to take a deep breath when I felt nothing but contempt. I was amenable when

I wanted to scream and passive-aggressive when morals and ethics were at risk. When it became clear that moral and ethical behavior was bankrupt I found another place, where I hoped there would be a culture I could support. Alas, as time passed history repeated itself. I smiled sweetly, gave a plausible explanation for my departure and moved on.

I left religious schools behind and found a position in a public school system. This was yet another institution where morals, ethics, and values were fed liberally to students but practiced sparingly among administrators and faculty.

I never found utopia. I didn't expect to. But I did expect that people, who were supposed to be reinforcing the concepts of goodness and good citizenship, would at least make the effort. I had learned that both public and private institutions, just as the businesses and organizations I had known, were corrupt. From my early twenties on I experienced decline in the goodness of the world around me.

Over the duration of my career I was reminded time and again that it is futile to work toward improvement when change is not possible. I engaged only where I perceived a positive outcome was possible and turned from toxic situations that would be addressed only when a crisis occurred. I learned to save my energy for the battles that just might, in the end, make a difference. In other words, do your best in your own sphere. Save yourself for the major disasters; the time and place where the positive may win the field.

There are those who have suggested that my approach reveals a lack of self-confidence. Perhaps, but I prefer to assess my course in terms of reality.

Starting a war that can bring only further destruction

rather than healing to people and/or institutions is counter productive.

Finally, I retired leaving the chaos. Perhaps, I thought, they would turn things around. But they didn't and I guess I shouldn't be surprised.

Eagles' Wings

"They will soar as with eagles' wings;
they will run and not grow weary,
walk and not grow faint."

Isaiah 40:31

Dad loved *On Eagles' Wings*. It was one of the hymns we sang during his funeral service. The hymn was inspired by the ninety-first psalm. But it also speaks to the quotation from Isaiah. Both give voice to the timeless yearning for meaning in our lives; for hope, peace, understanding and, finally, for consolation, comfort and solace in times of tragedy and loss.

Among all other birds, the eagle has inspired, intrigued, and frightened most peoples of the world. We know this from the stories that come to us from ancient times. In European myths eagles were deliverers from famine and seen as messengers for the Greek god Zeus.

Through human history the eagle has been a symbol

of divinity. Eagles' wings signify protection, their gripping talons the destruction of evildoers. The eagle's majestic bearing brought about its association with ancient rulers, for example the Persians, Babylonians and Romans. More contemporary nations as well have adopted the eagle as their symbol of power. Examples include Napoleon's empire and Nazi Germany. The eagle has been associated with the sun; Christian salvation, redemption, resurrection, and in the Middle Ages were often found on coats of arms.

In some archaic cultures the beating of eagles' wings was believed to create thunder. Among others its feathers stood for truth. Simply put, the eagle has influenced not only nature, but the beliefs and attitudes of humanity.

The eagle is a streamlined bird, finely shaped and sleek, an intelligent creature that, causes us to look into our minds, our intellects and gifts to evaluate where we are and where we might go. For me, what path do I follow? Where do my talents lie? What is the clearest channel to my best and most productive self? Do I stay the course or focus on life changing choices?

Jane Austin once wrote, "Everything nourishes what is already strong."

I exercise skills that maintain energy, that nourish my accomplishments and reinforce my competence. But I also know that growth starves and dies if not engaged in the unexplored, in opening the self to new possibilities. The process of personal development requires a broadening perspective, becoming aware of deeper spiritual and life affirming principles; of including more than my own ego in my world view.

Nourishing the strong may require only limited exertion. But to engage the starving one needs stamina. Just as eagles roost on mountain tops and high in the limbs of lifeless trees to observe their surroundings, so too I seek perspective and in so doing become aware of the changes up and down, to left and right, before and behind me. I watch for those changes and having perceived new possibilities I move on, reach out to feed mind and soul, and in the process, if possible, feed others that hunger.

The cycle of my experiences have four phases. In the beginning there is a *rippling*, a feeling that something is about to change. As sensitivity intensifies I ask myself, "What do I do, where do I go?" The answer? *Seeking*. The eagle's instincts may send it to another mountain top or dying tree limb, perhaps to a transient roost. For me, there is *contemplation* and whether I choose foolishly or wisely, I come to a *decision*, a new status quo. And I begin anew to wait for that rippling, the sense that my world is about to change yet again.

There are those who declare we have only *one* chance in life. I've found this may be true for some, invalid for others. The young have time; to reverse course, to experiment, to take varying paths. But as we grow older we may have little or no time to alter or atone for the end product of our choices. All of a life, with all its potential, its frustrations and celebrations, its sadness and triumphs comes together in the sum total of who you are, of who I am.

Like the eagle, I strive to rise above the fray to observe and to engage my curiosity. But unlike the eagle I create my own unique story.

The Rose Garden

"God gave us memories that we may have roses in December." J. M. Barrie

James Matthew Barrie was an author and dramatist. Among his works, he is best known for *Peter Pan*, the boy who refused to grow up. He counted among his friends G. K. Chesterton, A. A. Milne and Alfred Tennyson. He was born in Kirriemuir, Scotland, died of pneumonia June 19, 1937 and is buried in the place of his birth.

On May 3, 1922, Barrie was invited to deliver the Rectorial Address at Saint Andrew's University in his home country. In that address he said, "… I do not remember the great ones. In my experience … the people I have cared for most and who have seemed most worth caring for – my December roses – have been very simple folk…."

Barrie went on to say that there is nothing much, except courage, worth talking about to young people or "white-haired men and women." World War I was over, but Barrie urged both graduates and undergraduates in his audience to hold fast to courage. Another war was coming. Old men would send the young off to war once again.

The courage Barrie spoke of was physical courage; the ability to confront the enemy on a battlefield, to endure physical pain, hardship or the threat of death. But moral courage is different. It is the ability to distinguish between right and wrong, to understand and adhere to moral judgment and behavior in the face of disagreement, opposition, shame, scandal and humiliation. Moral courage requires the ability to withstand personal, social and emotional attacks that can bring about isolation, shunning and the possibility of physical harm.

Elizabeth Gilbert wrote, " Every man has an obscure respect for courage in others, especially if it is moral courage, the rarest and most difficult sort of bravery … It makes the very brute understand that this man is more than a man." And women, as well, who possess moral courage – among them Irena Sendlerowa, who saved Jewish children in World War II Poland and Taslima Nazreen known across the world for her writing and as a fighter for human rights. These women make the savage understand that they stand above others. They are December roses.

In our culture some say the opposite of courage is conformity. Others say it is cowardice, and still others fear or corruption. However we define it, courage is, whether we are conscious of it or not, part of our everyday lives. For me the person who recognizes, who feels that something is wrong and stands for right even though he/she is fearful of the consequences, is a courageous person.

I walk through the rose garden alive with the fragrance of blooms; red, yellow, pink, white. I reach for a perfect red flower and flinch as my thumb connects with a thorn hidden behind the rose. I take a tissue from my pocket and wipe the blood away. The rose hid the treachery of the thorn below. Courage, distracted by the sweetness in the air, the sight of perfect petals and vibrancy of color, diverts me from the thorns that I know can't be far away. In the end my attention has to be drawn to the thorns.

So it is with the decisions, the small and the consequential, that I face each day. Choosing avoidance in its many forms, or facing situations squarely, both have consequences. In the end, the voice in my head and/or the feeling in the pit of my stomach have come to be my measure of rightness, of truth. Or, to paraphrase Marcelle Mignault-Strong, *the memories of December roses are the good deeds done through life, the roses that brighten my "December."*

Hear the Water, Feel its Mood

" You could not step twice into the same rivers; for other waters are ever flowing on to you." Heraclitus of Ephesus

My sisters and I grew up in a 1937 housing development. Our home had three bedrooms, one bathroom and a siding of cypress and stucco. It had a large fenced yard half of which sloped down from a terrace.

Dad built a low safeguard of stone to prevent the soil in Mom's gardens from washing away in the heavy summer rains. Flowers bloomed on either side of steps he made to order in the hope that my sisters and I would use them rather than try to jump over or run through Mom's flowerbeds.

The area below the terrace seemed always to be damp or just plain wet, so Dad planted Weeping Willow trees (so called because of their long drooping branches, narrow leaves and ability to absorb vast amounts of water). Before long the *problem* was solved and forgotten.

Years later the trees stood tall. One of my sisters and I liked to climb the Willows. Each sat in the crook of a branch, swinging legs about and looking down on Mom's flowers and Mrs. Peters' vegetable garden and currant bushes.

One morning the sound of rain teeming in torrents drew me to the bedroom window. A fast growing, swift flowing *river* had taken possession of a wide swath of the yard.

I called to Mom, "There's a flood in the backyard. The willow trees can't hold the water anymore."

She smiled, "Don't worry; the water will go away when the rain stops."

But when the rain stopped the water remained.

"Mom, the water isn't going away."

"It will," she said in a cheerful tone.

"How do you know," I asked?

"A stream once flowed through our yard, and the yards of our neighbors. When it was decided the land would be used for houses, the stream was diverted, made to flow in a different path so the water wouldn't be a problem for us. We haven't seen this much water since your dad and I bought the house."

Mom didn't seem concerned. Her ease prompted calm. We stood by the window and watched the water race through the yard. There was nothing we could do but wait for the storm to run its course. And while time passed Mom read to us from our story books.

That was the last time I saw more than a small puddle in the yard. It wasn't until several years later that I learned to be cautious when dark clouds appeared in the sky and winds blew across my path.

§

Each July for several summers our family; Dad, Mom and daughters, packed up for a month long stay in a small cottage among the oak and maple trees beside Conesus

Lake in Western New York. We spent our days swimming, rowing the boat that came with the cottage, searching for wild strawberries and hiking wooded paths. In the evening we played games, told tales or sang songs, but whatever the activity there was always an atmosphere of fun and laughter.

Dad couldn't spend all those lovely days with us. He drove into the city each morning and returned each evening, usually carrying fresh tomatoes, ears of corn, or garden vegetables such as zucchini or green beans he purchased from roadside stands. Meals at the lake were always special. Sometimes Mom prepared the meal in the cottage while we sisters set the table, or helped Dad prepare fresh fish, or his own unique marinated chicken for the grill.

Dad went out in the row boat on weekends and some evenings after dinner to fish. But he rarely walked in the lake with us. You see, he had never learned to swim. But on a particularly hot day he might put on the bright yellow trunks he had bought because we wanted him to join us in the water. So fishing pole in hand he'd wade in up to his knees, drop his fish line and stay as he was until it was time for him to go into the cottage and read his newspaper.

§

As time passed I acquired a deepening understating of the place of water in my life as an individual and that of my family. As parents, one of us was always there; beside the bath tub, on the beach, next to the backyard wading pool.

Water sustained our family, provided relaxation, encouraged calm, defended us from summer's heat and quenched our thirst …

Water is the fluid without which we perish, yet its rage can deliver incomparable destruction. However it's formed, whatever its designation, wherever it travels, water touches the existence of every living thing.

I Wish …

"Dost thou love life? Then do not squander time, for that's the stuff life is made of." Benjamin Franklin

I wish, sometimes, that I were young again. In youth there were no aching fingers when I woke and I didn't fall asleep long before the party was over. There was a bounce in my walk and a devil-take-the-hindmost tilt to my head. I didn't have to be conscious of bending my knees when picking up our children as I do now with my grandchildren. My back didn't whisper warnings after only an hour of weeding the garden. Sleep came later and I woke refreshed earlier. As the seasons passed, I knew there was canning to be done and clothes to be made before school started. Dresses with ruffled skirts and blouses with rounded collars, pants with patch pockets and padded knees fell, as if by magic, from my sewing machine.

As fruits ripened jams and jellies went into glass jars, vegetables into the freezer. As winter approached venison was butchered, sausage made, apple sauce and apple butter preserved.

Above all, as the day came to a close, when the children were in bed and my love sat reading, I sat beside him darning socks, hemming a small pair of pants, or smocking a pint-sized blouse. I knew my world was an impregnable fortress; my life and family safe and secure. The frailties and insecurities of others and of other spheres were not of my world.

As the years pass I have come to understand that black and white are an illusion of the young. In truth, there are only infinite shades of gray. For the fortunate, wisdom takes the place of bombast and certitude. Although loathed, it is easier to accept the frailties of the body than to affirm the reality of one's impotence in controlling life's events, for ourselves certainly, for our children tragically, since they lack the experience of age.

Yet the deeper one travels into the labyrinth of age the clearer it becomes that rationality gives each of us choices: to bemoan the passing of youth, or to experience the sheer joy of the cognizance of age.

In youth a woman finds her essence in the extension of other beings. With age comes a self-assurance born of knowledge rather than of naiveté. I am comfortable with myself. The aged woman feels herself a being that stands alone, apart, complete in herself.

Insight and perspective accompany age permitting the chronology of a lifetime to be arrayed in a kind of vista that accepts the blunders of one's existence while extolling the masterpieces of that same epoch. Insight and perspective converge with the art of gracious acceptance.

I am content, though there may still be challenges that call to me; *other worlds to conquer, other mountains to climb.* If so, there are those like me who would embrace yet another opportunity to view firsthand what had not been previously seen.

On holidays and weekends in summer the author often stayed with grandparents. At home, she sat with her father to hear tales of Dad's youth. As she grew she found herself writing of family incidents she had been told. Through time images continued to settle in Virginia Ward's plentiful library. There were books of grandchild memoirs, and writing guides for the young and the mature.

Labyrinths reach into prehistory and have no geographic cultural, or religious limit. As medieval times passed, labyrinths fell into disuse. In recent times labyrinths have emerged as spiritual tools, a modern mode of worship and have brought with them a sense of peace, comfort and rest as one walks the labyrinth's path, stops to meditate, reflect or think deeply.

authorHOUSE®

ISBN 978-1-4772-6747-9

51295

9 781477 267479